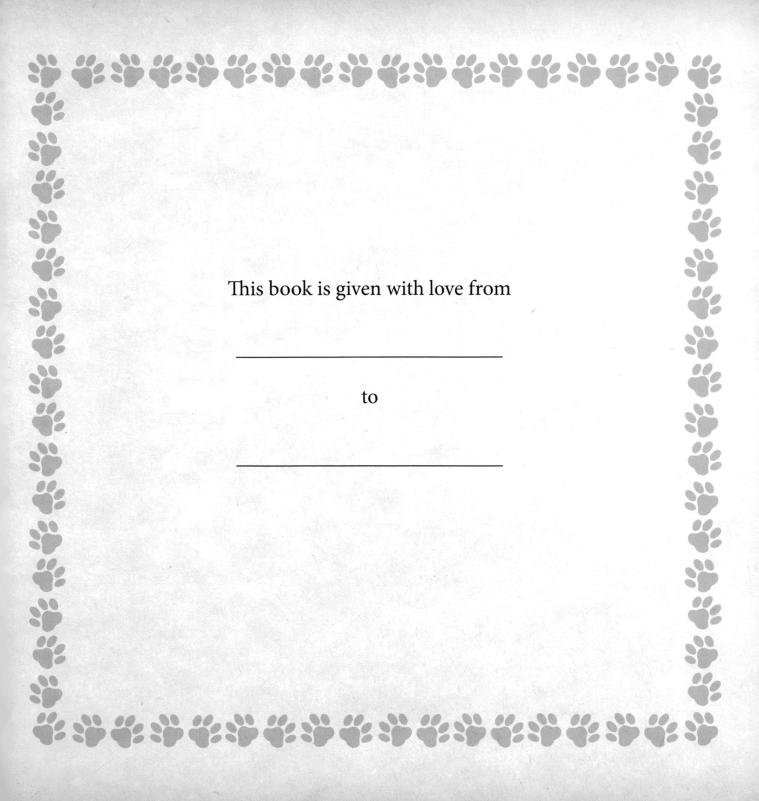

This book is given with love from

_____

to

_____

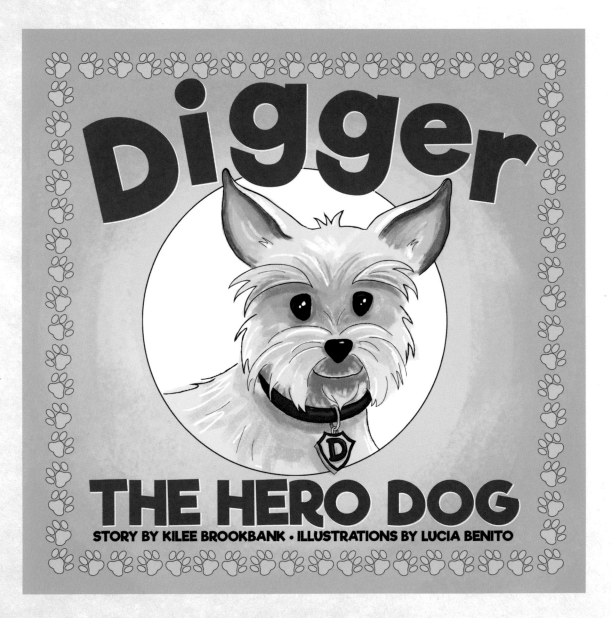

Digger

THE HERO DOG

STORY BY KILEE BROOKBANK · ILLUSTRATIONS BY LUCIA BENITO

KiCam
PROJECTS

Cover and book design by Mark Sullivan

ISBN 978-0-6928975-7-7 (paperback)
ISBN 978-0-9991581-9-7 (hardback)

Printed in the United States of America

Published by KiCam Projects

www.KiCamProjects.com

For Digger, Doogie, and Dori, plus
all the other animal friends who
make our families complete.

And to all the heroes and future
heroes among us, remember:
Anyone, no matter how big or how
small, can make a difference!

My name is Digger,
and Kilee is my best friend.
We have always been buddies
and will be 'til the end.

One day I heard a loud boom
caused by a fiery spark.
Kilee had been knocked out,
so I ran to her and began to bark.

I woke her up,
and she got off the floor.
Our home was on fire,
and we ran for the door.

As we got outside,
I could tell she was hurt.
Her clothes were on fire,
and I knew she was burnt.

We ran to the neighbors,
who poured water on her hair.
They put the fire out,
but Kilee needed more care.

The fire department was coming fast,
with big engines churning.
Kilee needed an ambulance,
and our house was still burning.

I was circling around her
and barking very loud.
There was black smoke in the air,
like a big, dark cloud.

"Please help my friend,"
I was trying to say.
I was scared for her life;
it was a very sad day.

Kilee went to Shriners Hospital,

where they treat kids with burns.

They are the best in the world,

as I'm sure you have heard.

She was gone for a long time
having surgeries and more.
I couldn't wait to see her
as I waited by the door.

After thirty-eight days,
Kilee was beginning to heal.
With everything she had been through,
it was a really big deal.

We built a new house
and we're all back together.
I'm still Kilee's protector,
and I'm busier than ever.

I watch over my family—
there's no better place to be.
Home sweet home
for Kilee and me.

About the Author

Kilee Brookbank is a college student, shoe fanatic, animal lover—and burn survivor. Severely injured when a gas leak caused her house to explode in November 2014, Kilee was hospitalized for thirty-eight days before returning home to a life of new challenges and a new "normal." Kilee, who attends Xavier University, wrote the award-winning *Beautiful Scars* in 2016 and is the founder of the Kilee Gives Back Foundation. Her inspiring story has been featured by *The Doctors, Inside Edition,* MTV, *Seventeen, Girls' Life, Woman's World,* and *Redbook.*

Grateful to Digger

Thanks to Digger, Kilee enjoys a happy life full of love with her beautiful blended family, from left: stepbrother Houstin, brother Cameron (holding Doogie), stepbrother Collin, mom Lori (holding Dori), stepdad Wade, stepmom Brooke, sister Carter, and dad Jason.

Be Prepared!

To protect yourself and your family, create an escape plan in the event of a fire or gas leak in your home and practice it together. Learn two ways out of every room and agree on a meeting place outside.

If you find yourself in a fire, here's what to do:
- If you're in a room with a closed door, do NOT open the door if you see smoke under it.
- If you don't see smoke, check the handle. If it is hot, do not open the door.
- If you can open the door, and there is no smoke or heat, hurry to your planned exit.
- Stay low to the ground as you exit.
- If you can't get out right away, yell for help and call 911. Do NOT hide in a closet or under a bed.

Learn more at:
beburnaware.org and shrinershospitalsforchildren.org

Be Aware!

Energy companies add an unpleasant smell to natural gas and propane to help families identify dangerous leaks. You might notice a foul odor similar to sulfur, rotten eggs, a skunk's spray, or a dead animal.

Scratch and sniff the sticker below to learn what natural gas and propane smell like. If you smell this in your home, tell an adult and get out of the house right away!

Do not use lights, appliances, phones, or cell phones. These items can produce small flames or sparks that could trigger an explosion.

Run outside and call for help from a safe location.

Burn and Fire Awareness

Shriners Hospitals for Children offer some smart ways both adults and kids can prevent burns and fires:

- Install smoke detectors near each bedroom and at the top of each stairway.
- Treat matches and lighters as tools—not toys!
- Learn the smells caused by natural gas or propane leaks, which signal danger.
- Use electrical outlet covers.
- Never leave food unattended while cooking, and be sure to turn pot handles inward. Also remember to use oven mitts and pot holders.
- Store all chemicals and cleaners out of reach of children and/or keep those storage cabinets locked.
- Do not leave lighted candles unattended.
- Always supervise children in the bath to prevent scalding.
- Unplug electrical appliances when they're not in use.
- Do not place electrical cords or wires under rugs or in high-traffic areas.
- Have fireplaces and chimneys inspected every year before use.
- Have electrical wiring inspected professionally every ten years.

Learn more at:
beburnaware.org and shrinershospitalsforchildren.org

Beautiful Scars

Do you want to know more about Kilee Brookbank's inspiring story?

Then check out *Beautiful Scars: A Life Redefined*, written by Kilee and her mom, Lori Highlander. *Beautiful Scars* is available now at KiCamProjects.com and Amazon.com.

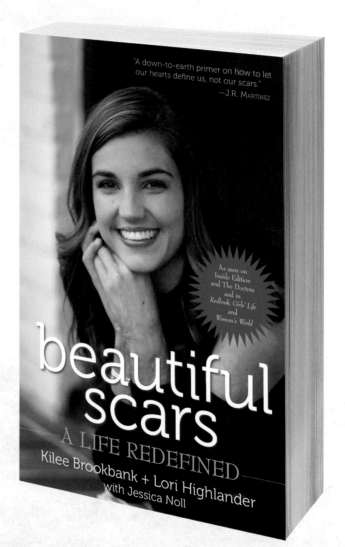

Who's Digger Helping Now?

Digger and Kilee are proud to support two organizations close to their hearts:

Shriners Hospitals for Children
Shriners Hospitals provide the highest-quality care to children with neuromusculoskeletal conditions, burn injuries, and other special healthcare needs without regard to the ability of a patient or family to pay.

Shriners Hospitals serve twenty-two locations in the United States, Canada, and Mexico, including burn-care units in Cincinnati; Boston; Galveston, Texas; Sacramento, Calif.; and Pasadena, Calif.

To learn more about the hospitals' services or to find a location, please visit shrinershospitalsforchildren.org.

K9s For Warriors
K9s For Warriors is dedicated to providing service canines to warriors suffering from post-traumatic stress disability, traumatic brain injury, and/or military sexual trauma as a result of military service post-9/11. K9s For Warriors is especially important to Kilee, whose grandfather Edward Adams is a Vietnam veteran and a double amputee.

To learn more, visit www.k9sforwarriors.org.

Kilee Gives Back
FOUNDATION

The Kilee Gives Back Foundation was formed in 2015 by Kilee Brookbank and her family to pay forward the community's kindness and generosity through events and fundraisers that benefit Shriners Hospitals for Children-Cincinnati.

 In its first two years, the foundation raised more than $200,000 for Shriners Cincinnati.

To learn more or to donate, please visit KileeGivesBack.org.